THE
Aspiring Artist's
STUDIO

Beaded Jewelry

THE
Aspiring Artist's
STUDIO

Beaded Jewelry

Tair Parnes

Sterling Publishing Co., Inc.
New York

Designed by Eddie Goldfine
Layout by Ariane Rybski
Edited by Shoshana Brickman
Photography by Matt Cohen

Library of Congress Cataloging-in-Publication Data Available

2 4 6 8 10 9 7 5 3 1

Published by Sterling Publishing Co., Inc.
387 Park Avenue South, New York, NY 10016
© 2007 by Penn Publishing Ltd.
Distributed in Canada by Sterling Publishing
c/o Canadian Manda Group, 165 Dufferin Street,
Toronto, Ontario, Canada M6K 3H6
Distributed in the United Kingdom by GMC Distribution Services,
Castle Place, 166 High Street, Lewes, East Sussex, England BN7 1XU
Distributed in Australia by Capricorn Link (Australia) Pty. Ltd.
P.O. Box 704, Windsor, NSW 2756, Australia

Sterling ISBN-13: 978-1-4027-3259-1
ISBN-10: 1-4027-3259-7

For information about custom editions, special sales, premium and
corporate purchases, please contact Sterling Special Sales
Department at 800-805-5489 or specialsales@sterlingpub.com.

Introduction

Does your eye for fashion extend beyond the selection at your local shopping mall? Do jewelry counters ignite your imagination? If so, beading is the perfect craft for you! Few things satisfy a craving for self-expression quite like working with beads. Not only that, but the repetitive nature of beading has a meditative quality that is soothing and relaxing. Beading is an excellent chance to make distinct jewelry that is uniquely your own, and a wonderful way to wind down after a busy day. It keeps your fingers busy while your imagination runs free.

Beads come in a multitude of shapes, sizes, styles, and colors. They may be plain or fancy, large or small, glass or wood. If you can drill a hole in it, you can make a bead out of it. The possibilities are endless.

In one form or another, beads have made a recurring appearance in many fashion phases. There was the string of pearls worn by flappers in the 1920s; the bead-studded decade of the 1960s; the trend for Tibetan beads in the 1990s. Traditional Native American art and jewelry has always made use of colorful beads; indeed, indigenous cultures all over the world have used beads in decorations and jewelry for thousands of years.

Clearly, beads are not a passing fad. While beading techniques and compositions may change over time, beads themselves never go out of style. Their enduring popularity is a testament to the tiny bead's great power to embody culture, express style, and suit every personality.

These days, specialty bead shops and craft stores are popping up all over the place, so finding beads in your neighborhood shouldn't be a problem. There is also an abundance of bead resources available online, enabling you to order a wide variety of beads directly to your front door.

Aspiring Artist's Studio: Beaded Jewelry Design takes you on a colorful journey into a world of infinite artistic possibilities. Artist and author Tair Parnes guides you through twenty-three projects, clearly described with step-by-step instructions and accompanied by vibrant color photos. Every earring, necklace, brooch, and bracelet is like a little exhibition of contemporary art plucked from her studio.

Tair brings a world of inspiration and experience to her craft. Trained in art forms ranging from tapestry to jewelry making, classic painting to modern fashion design, she travels the world learning about international techniques, styles, and color combinations. The result is a unique collection of projects ranging from simple earrings suitable for daily wear to elegant bracelets for very special occasions. All projects are easily adaptable, allowing you to make beaded jewelry that is a distinct expression of your own taste.

Tools and Materials

The tools and materials used in these beading projects are basic and can be found in most bead shops and craft stores. The Internet is also an excellent source for ordering materials; if you live in an area that doesn't have many craft stores, ordering online may be the easiest way to find what you need.

When it comes to buying beads, there's no telling where you may find something that catches your eye. Bead stores, craft shows, garage sales, flea markets, the Internet, and trips abroad are all wonderful opportunities for finding beautiful and unusual beads. Be warned, though! The large variety of beads can overwhelm even the most decisive shopper.

Tools

Beading needles ease the process of stringing beads by pulling the thread—often a double strand—through the small holes of the beads. Given the tiny diameter of bead holes, beading needles have to be very thin. They are sized by number: the higher the number, the thinner the needle. The most suitable needles for the projects in this book are size 11 or 12, which are slim needles with particularly thin eyes.

Round-nose pliers, aptly named for their round end, are used to make circles and loops in eye pins and head pins. These pliers come in various sizes. I recommend using larger pliers for large loops and smaller pliers for more delicate projects.

Scissors vary according to their purpose. Fabric-cutting scissors are best for cutting Lycra and other fabric, but fingernail scissors will suffice for cutting thread. Just remember that the thinner the material, the gentler the scissors should be.

Wire cutters are used to cut wire in a precise and clean manner. They come in several sizes; the thicker the wire, the sturdier the cutters need to be.

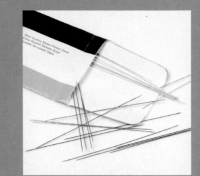

Beading needles

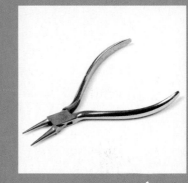

Round-nose pliers

Scissors

Wire cutters

Materials

Beads are available in a vast array of colors, shapes, sizes, materials, and prices. Take your pick of crystal, wood, metal, acrylic, stone, plastic, or pearl! Choose between round, teardrop, faceted, square, and tube-shaped! Or why not use all of the above? Envision a rainbow of colors, and don't hesitate to incorporate other types of beads in any of the projects in this book. In fact, you may find some designs suit you even better when you combine various bead types, colors, and sizes. Since variety is what makes each of these projects unique, feel free to bring your own style to every single one of them. The projects in this book use the following types of beads:

Cloisonné beads are delicate enamel beads made by soldering partitions onto a metal bead. The spaces between the partitions are then filled with various colors of enamel. Although the name comes from the French word for partition, *cloison*, Chinese artisans are the masters of the craft today.

Shell beads and buttons may be made from a variety of materials including cowrie shell, mother of pearl, and paua shell. They come in various shapes and sizes and add a delicate elegance to beaded jewelry. The projects in this book use undecorated flat white shell beads and buttons, but feel free to integrate colored shell, or use shell that is carved or engraved with simple designs and patterns.

Cloisonné beads

shell beads

shell buttons

Glass beads come in vibrant colors, diverse shapes, and a wide range of sizes. Lampwork beads are handmade using a blowtorch and rods of colored glass. Millefiori is another technique used to make glass beads. These beads are made from the fusion of several glass rods together. The rods are then sliced and melted over a glass core. Pressed glass beads are made by pouring the glass into a mold. They can be shaped and imprinted, and are easily mass produced. Most of the projects in this book use lampwork beads; they are often sold in assorted packages, giving you a maximum selection of styles.

Seed beads are small, round beads that are usually measured in millimeters and sized by number: the higher the number, the smaller the bead. The projects in this book call for three sizes of seed beads: size 11, which has a diameter of 2 millimeters, size 8, which has a diameter of 3 millimeters, and size 6, which has a diameter of 4 millimeters.

While seed beads may all seem similar at first glance, they actually come in an astonishingly wide array of colors and styles, and with several different types of finish. Translucent beads allow light to shine through. They may be **silver-lined**, **copper-lined**, **bronze-lined**, or **color-lined**, qualities which subtly alter the appearance of the bead. **Opaque** beads don't allow any light to shine through at all; they generally have a single, solid color. As for finishes, **matte** beads have a dull finish while **glossy**, **silk**, and **pearl** beads all have shiny finishes. Beads classified as having an **aurora borealis** or **AB** finish are all slightly different in color; they are also called **iris** or **rainbow** beads. **Metallic** and **galvanized** beads have shiny, metallic finishes.

glass beads

Seed beads

Appliqués are small pillows that come in many different shapes and sizes. They are sold in craft stores and hobby shops, usually in the textile or sewing section. While you can make your own small pillow by sewing together two pieces of fabric and filling it with a little stuffing, store-bought appliqués are a time-saving alternative. Once covered in beads, it's hard to tell the difference between handmade pillows and store-bought appliqués.

Appliqués

Beading thread must be very thin, so that it can easily enter the holes in small beads—sometimes two or three times. Make sure the beading thread you choose is strong, so that the finished piece is durable.

For those of you overwhelmed by the process of choosing beads, take heart! Selecting beading thread is much simpler. It comes in a variety of colors; simply choose a color that is similar to or lighter than the beads you will be using. For projects that require you to use two or more threads at the same time, it may help to use different colors of beading thread so that you can distinguish between them.

Beading thread also comes in a variety of widths; choose a width that is thin enough to fit into the smallest bead in your project. If you are using only large beads in a project, use thicker beading thread, as this will make your jewelry more durable. **Beading thread should not be confused with sewing thread**, which snaps easily and discolors quickly. Remember to use high quality beading thread as this will increase the durability of your project.

Beading thread

Lycra is used as a base in several of the projects. It is the ideal fabric for making these pieces of jewelry because it is durable, flexible, and can easily be stretched. Glimpses of fabric may be visible in the finished product, so choose a color that complements the beads in your project.

Jewelry findings are the metal items that help make the finished piece of jewelry. These vital components are made of various materials, including sterling silver, gold, and pewter. When choosing your jewelry findings, be sure to select ones that are of high quality, as you don't want them to rust or break while you are wearing your jewelry.

Clasps are those things we all fiddle with when putting on and taking off necklaces and bracelets. They come in a wide variety of shapes and sizes —choose one that goes well with your design. While some projects use store-bought clasps, others include instructions for making your own clasp.

Ear wires are necessary for turning your beaded masterpieces into earrings. Small hoop earrings can also be used to support beaded earrings.

Clasps

Ear wires

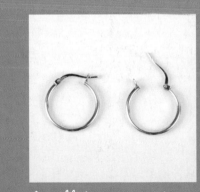

Small hoop earrings

Eye pins are pins with a loop at one end. The loop prevents beads from falling off, and provides an eye for attaching thread.

Head pins are pins with a flat head at one end to prevent beads from falling off.

Jump rings are connector rings that are available open, closed, and in different diameters. They are often necessary for connecting clasps to beaded jewelry.

Pin backs are used for making pendants and brooches. When affixing a pin back to the back of a project, make sure that it's not visible from the front.

Glue strengthens and reinforces knots. Liquid superglue is most suitable since it pours slowly and only a small amount is needed. Superglue can also make threading the needles easier. Simply dip the end of your thread into the glue, let it dry for a few moments until stiff, then poke the thread through the eye of the needle.

Round shoelace or thin rope is used as a base for some necklaces. If you have a particularly lovely piece of fabric, you can roll it tightly into a thin cylinder, sew the seam, and use it as a base for a necklace.

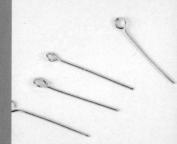

Eye pins

Head pins

Jump rings

Pin backs

Rubber beading thread is perfect for making bracelets without clasps, as it allows them to be put on and taken off easily. Be sure to use rubber thread that is strong, thick, transparent, yet thin enough to fit into the thinnest beads you've chosen for your project.

Thin flexible wire is concealed inside cylinders of fabric to add support for shaped pieces of jewelry.

Straight pins hold fabric in place while sewing the seams of cylinders. Although straight pins may not be necessary for making short cylinders, they can help keep longer cylinders tightly wrapped as you sew.

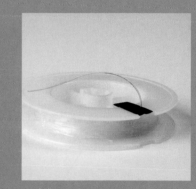

Rubber beading thread

Tips

Here are some general tips to keep in mind as you bead.

• If you're having difficulty threading tiny-eyed beading needles, try cutting your thread at an angle and moistening the end with a little water or glue. While this method isn't foolproof, it helps stiffen the thread and often makes sliding it into the eye much easier.

• A technique to make delicate seed bead branches is used in several projects. For step-by-step photos of this technique, see Cloisonné Cone Earrings (42 to 45).

• Some of the bracelets in this book (62 to 79) use regular beading thread and clasps; others use rubber beading thread. You can alter any design to use either type of thread. If you use regular beading thread, leave enough room on either side for attaching the jump ring and clasp. If you use rubber beading thread, make sure the thread is durable, and thin enough to fit through the smallest bead in your project.

• Some of the advanced projects in this book (102 to 123) include instructions for handmade clasps. Feel free to substitute store-bought clasps instead. Alternately, you may want to substitute one of the handmade clasps for a store-bought one in any of the other projects.

- Adjust the length of any necklace to make it as long or as short as you like. Although dimensions may differ for every person, here are some standard sizes to guide you. Chokers fit around the neck; they usually measure 14 to 16 inches. Princess necklaces rest below the collar bone; they are usually 19 inches long. Opera necklaces fall just above the waist; they generally measure 28 to 32 inches. Lariat necklaces can be wrapped around the neck several times; they may be 48 inches or longer.

- If you are making a short necklace, be sure to leave enough thread on either end for attaching the clasp.

- When making bracelets, it's particularly important that the size is just right, so measure against your wrist as you work.

- Pieces of tinsel made from decorated headpins are used in a number of projects. If you have trouble keeping them on the thread as you string them, try tying the thread in a loose, temporary knot. The knot should be big enough to stop the tinsel from sliding, but not so secure that you have trouble removing it when it comes time to tie both ends of the thread together.

Note from the Author

Few things are as rewarding as making your own beaded jewelry. Wearing it yourself—or giving it as gifts to close friends and family—provides a wonderful feeling of satisfaction and pleasure.

Using this book

The projects in this book are organized from easiest to most challenging. Projects in the first four sections include detailed instructions and photographs of key steps. I recommend starting out with a few of these projects; once you are familiar with the basics, move on to the fifth section, Advanced Projects. These projects draw upon the techniques described in the first four chapters, but are more elaborate and require a little more experience. They also provide plenty of opportunities for innovation and adaptation—perfect for people who have mastered the basics.

Enjoying the Process

The pleasure in beading isn't just in the final product; it's also part of the creative process. Take your time selecting just the right beads, and choose colors that make you feel good. Once you're familiar with the techniques, you'll find the beading process becomes rhythmic, soothing, and relaxing.

Symmetry

One of the great things about creating your own jewelry is that you can make it to suit your style exactly. If you like your earrings to be identical, note the number of beads in the first earring and duplicate it in the second. If you prefer your earrings to be a little different, that's fine too. Personally, I like partial symmetry in earrings—I may use similar colors in different compositions, or different colors in similar compositions. When it comes to necklaces and bracelets, you can make the elements identical in size or color, or subtly different. Do whatever works for you to create jewelry that is an expression of your distinct style.

Improvisation and adaptation

Feel free to improvise and adapt every project by using different colors and diverse types of beads. Once you have mastered the basic techniques, try modifying the designs too.

Adjusting sizes

Please note that all of the sizes in these projects are estimates, and quite generous. If you have a small wrist or prefer to wear shorter necklaces, adjust the length of the jewelry accordingly.

Practice makes perfect

Don't be frustrated if some of these techniques take a long time at the beginning. They require practice and patience, so relax, enjoy the process, and rest assured that after a few tries, you'll get the hang of it.

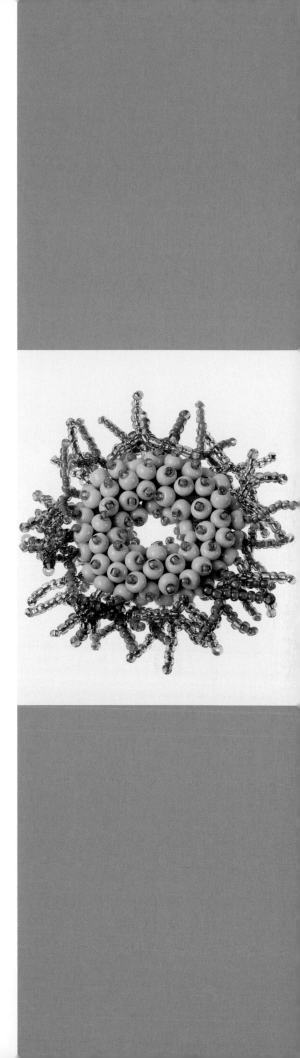

necklaces

Nothing completes an outfit like the perfect necklace. Extend the length of any design to make an opera-length necklace or shorten to make a choker.

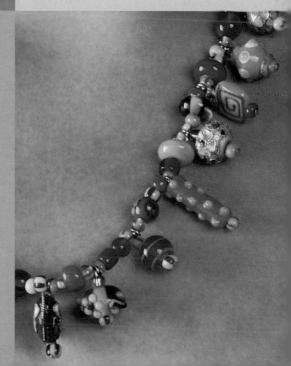

Tinsel Necklace

This festive necklace is a great way to show off colorful glass beads. Incorporating enamel, crystal, and precious stone beads will add even more twinkle to the tinsel.

Materials

Thirty-five 1-inch head pins

Glass beads, variety of shapes and colors

Bead thread

Superglue

Seed beads, size 11, variety of colors

Jump rings

Clasp

Tools

Round-nose pliers

Wire cutters

Scissors

A

Directions

1 To make a piece of tinsel, string 2–4 glass beads on a head pin. Use round-nose pliers to bend the sharp end of the head pin into a closed loop and use wire cutters to cut off any remaining wire. Combine a variety of shapes and colors on each pin, so that each piece of tinsel is a little different (Figure A). Repeat to make 35 pieces of tinsel.

2 Cut a 40-inch piece of thread. Dip one end of the thread in superglue and set aside to dry. When the glue dries, the thread will be stiff and easy to thread.

(continued on page 26)

3 String 8 seed beads onto the thread and draw them along until they are about 1 inch from the other end of the thread. Pass the beads through a jump ring and clasp and draw the two ends of thread together to make a ring of beads that encircles the jump ring. Tie a double knot to secure the ring of beads, and reinforce with a dot of superglue (Figure B). Wait for the super-glue to dry, then cut the shorter end of the thread close to the knot.

4 String 3–4 glass beads onto the thread, then string 1 piece of tinsel. Repeat until the necklace is the right length (Figure C).

5 To finish, string 8 seed beads onto the thread and pass through a jump ring. Draw the 8 beads into a ring that encircles the jump ring and tie a double knot to secure (Figure D). Reinforce the knot with a dot of superglue. Wait for the superglue to dry, then cut the end of the thread close to the knot.

B

C

D

Bead and Button Necklace

This necklace is a great opportunity for mixing colors, shapes, and sizes of beads and buttons. I used shell buttons in this design, but any small buttons will look lovely.

Materials

Beading thread

Seed beads, size 11, variety of colors

Glass beads, variety of shapes and colors

10–15 pairs of shell buttons, variety of sizes and shapes

Superglue

Tools

Beading needle, size 11 or 12

Scissors

Directions

1 Thread the needle with triple the length of thread of the desired necklace, double it, and tie both ends together.

2 String a seed bead to prevent the larger beads from falling off the thread, then string several glass beads.

3 String a 4-hole button by drawing the needle out the front of one buttonhole. String 2–4 seed beads, then insert the needle into the diagonal buttonhole. Orient a matching button so that the two buttons are back-to-back and string it in a similar manner (Figures A1 and A2). Pull the thread out from between the two buttons and draw the needle out through an empty button-hole on the first button. String 2–4 seed beads, then insert the needle on a diagonal. Repeat on the other button, then pull the thread out from between the two buttons so that they are very close together (Figure B).

(continued on page 30)

4 Continue stringing glass beads and back-to-back pairs of buttons (Figure C). There is no need to be consistent in the number or type of glass beads between each pair of buttons, as variety is part of this necklace's charm. Incorporating 2-hole buttons and stringing 4-hole buttons with parallel rather than diagonal rows of beads are other options for adding variety.

5 To finish, tie both ends of the thread together in a double knot and reinforce with a dot of superglue. Wait for the superglue to dry, then cut the thread close to the knot.

C

Triangle Necklace

One glance at this necklace and you'll know that triangles aren't just for geometry class. The directions call for two different colors of beading thread, but this is more for clarity than for decorative purposes.

Materials

Beading thread, white and red

Pair of jump rings

Clasp

Seed beads, size 11, variety of colors

Glass beads, variety of shapes and colors

40 flat shell beads

Superglue

Tools

Scissors

2 beading needles, size 11 or 12

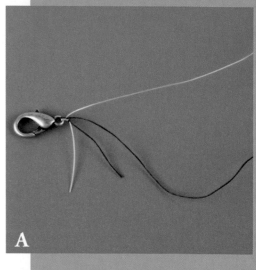

Directions

1 Cut a 63-inch piece of white thread and a 39-inch piece of red thread. Tie the threads together at one end and attach to a jump ring and clasp (Figure A). Thread each needle with a different color thread.

2 String 3–4 beads on both threads as if they were a single thread.

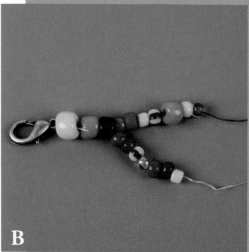

3 String 5–7 beads on the red thread and 5–7 beads on the white thread to make two sides of the triangle. You'll be using beads of various sizes, so make sure that the length of each side is even (Figure B).

(continued on page 34)

4 To make the third side of the triangle, string a shell bead followed by a seed bead on the white thread. Loop the thread around the seed bead and draw it back through the shell bead. String another shell bead and seed bead in the same manner.

5 Draw the thread between the two shell beads so that they are back-to-back, then go back through the bead that is adjacent to the first shell bead. String 5–6 beads onto the white thread to make the third side of the triangle. Remember to make this side even with the other two sides.

6 To close the triangle, string one bead on both threads as if they were a single thread (Figure C).

7 Repeat steps 3–6 to make about 20 triangles, or as many as you'll need for your necklace.

C

8 To finish, string 3–4 seed beads on both threads as if they were a single thread, then tie a knot. Attach a jump ring to the end with a knot and reinforce with a dot of superglue. Wait for the superglue to dry, then cut the thread close to the knot and attach a clasp.

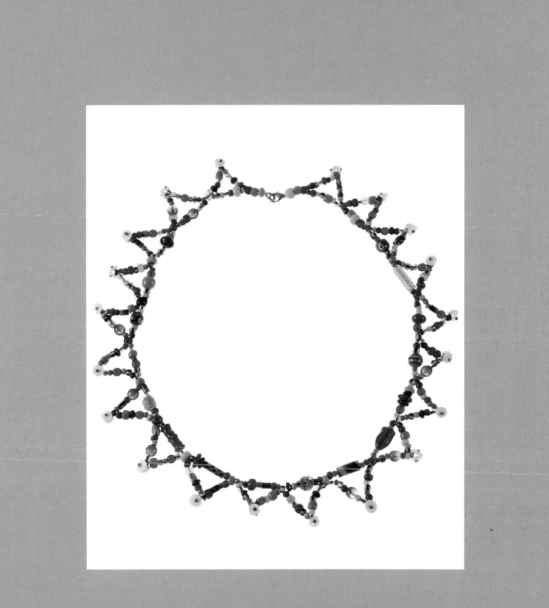

Porcupine Ball Necklace

Have a ball creating this effervescent necklace! Play around with different color combinations and don't shy away from using matte, glossy, and color-lined beads.

Materials

Beading thread

Fourteen 2½-inch squares of Lycra

Seed beads, size 6, variety of colors

Seed beads, size 11, variety of colors

Tools

Beading needle, size 11 or 12

Scissors

Directions

1 Thread the needle with a comfortable length of thread, double it, and tie both ends together.

2 Fold a piece of Lycra in half into a rectangle, then in half to make a small square. Fold all four corners into the middle of the square to make a smaller square, and sew the corners together (Figure A). Continue to fold and sew opposite corners into the middle, stretching and shaping the Lycra as you go (Figure B), until you have a small ball (Figure C). Repeat to make 14 balls, or as many as you'll need to make your necklace.

(continued on page 38)

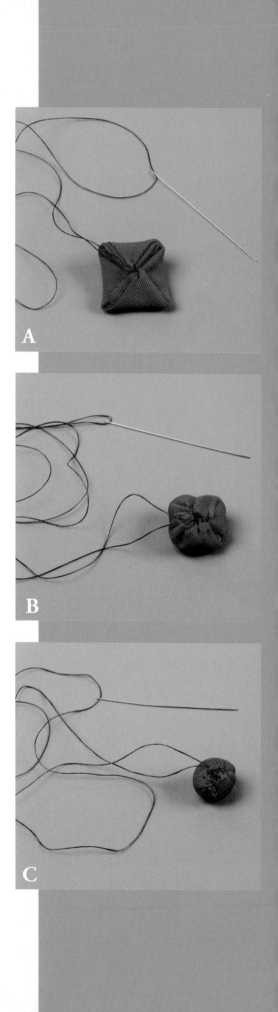

A

B

C

3 Insert the needle through a ball and string a large bead of one color followed by a small bead of a different color. Loop the thread around the small bead, draw it back through the larger bead, and insert into the ball. Push the needle out close to the newly attached beads and pull gently to secure against the fabric (Figure D).

4 Repeat step 3 until the whole ball is covered with beads, then tie a secure knot close to the ball and cut the thread.

5 Repeat steps 3–4, using different combinations of colors, to cover all 14 balls in beads.

6 Thread the needle with a 63-inch piece of thread. Double it and tie both ends together.

7 Insert the needle through a beaded ball, and push it out on the opposite side. String 35 small beads, then insert the needle into the next ball (Figure E).

8 Continue to string beaded balls and small beads until the necklace is the right length.

9 To finish, draw the thread out of the last ball, string 35 small beads, then insert it into the first ball. Push it out on the opposite side of the first ball and pull gently to secure. Tie a knot close to the ball and cut the thread.

D

E

Earrings

With these decorative designs dangling from your ears, you'll dress up even the simplest outfit.

Cloisonné Cone Earrings

Cloisonné is a colorful and delicate metalworking technique used to make vases, jewelry, and beads. Cloisonné beads can be purchased in many bead shops and online, but if you're having trouble finding them, any cone-shaped beads are fine.

Materials

Beading thread

Two 2-inch eye pins

Superglue

Seed beads, size 11, red, orange, pink

2 cone-shaped cloisonné beads

Pair of ear wires

Tools

Beading needle, size 11 or 12

Scissors

Round-nose pliers

Wire cutters

Directions

1 Thread the needle with a comfortable length of thread, double it, and tie both ends together. For these earrings, I suggest working with a piece of thread that is about 36 inches long, so that you can make all the branches on one earring without having to start a new thread.

2 Tie the knotted end of the thread to the ring of the eye pin and fasten with a drop of superglue (Figure A). Make a branch of beads by stringing 15 red beads, skipping over the last bead, and going back through 7 beads (Figure B).

(continued on page 44)

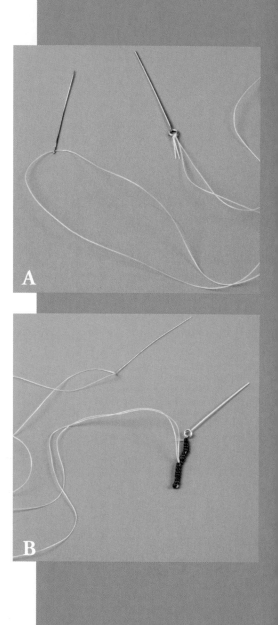

3 Gently pull the beads taut. Make a twig on the branch by stringing 10 red beads, skipping over the last bead, and going back through 7 beads (Figure C). Gently pull the beads taut. Make another twig by stringing 15 red beads, skipping over the last bead, and going back through 7 beads.

4 String 7 red beads, skip over the last bead, and go back through 6 beads. Draw the thread back through the beads that make up the base of the branch, so that it comes out next to the ring of the eye pin. Gently pull the thread taut and knot it around the ring (Figure D).

5 Repeat steps 3–4 using orange and pink beads (Figure E). Continue making branches until you have several branches of each color. After finishing the last branch, tie the thread to the ring and reinforce with a drop of superglue. Wait for the superglue to dry, then cut the thread close to the knot.

6 Thread a cone-shaped bead onto the eye pin so that the sharp end of the eye pin extends beyond the hole in the narrow end of the bead, and the beaded branches extend beyond the wide end of the bead. Use round-nose pliers to bend the sharp end of the eye pin into a ring and cut off any excess metal with wire cutters (Figure F).

7 Repeat steps 1–6 to make the second earring.

8 To finish, attach ear wires to the rings you made at the top of the eye pins.

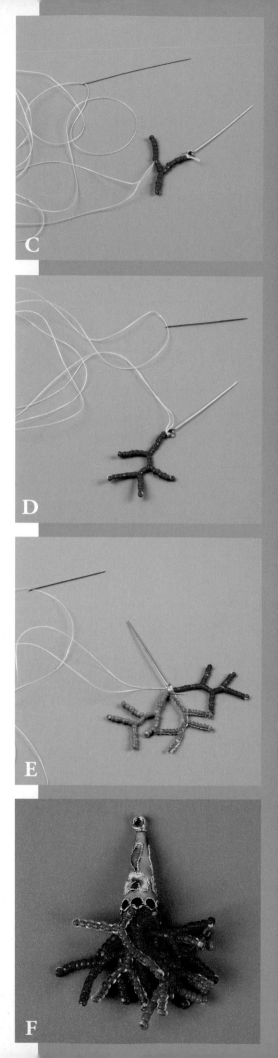

Fringed Earrings

Elegant yet fun, these earrings are a perfect way to accentuate a pair of beautiful large beads by setting them off against smaller ones.

Materials

Beading thread

Pair of small metal rings

2 large glass beads, maximum ½-inch diameter

Seed beads, size 11, orange and red

Superglue

Pair of ear wires

Tools

Beading needle, size 11 or 12

Scissors

Directions

1 Thread the needle with a comfortable length of thread, double it, and tie both ends together.

2 Tie the knotted end of the thread to a metal ring (Figure A).

3 String one of the large beads onto the thread until it is flush against the ring (Figure B).

(continued on page 48)

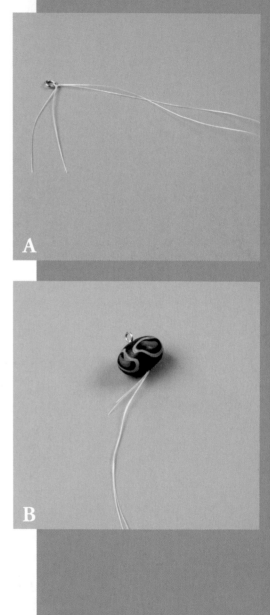

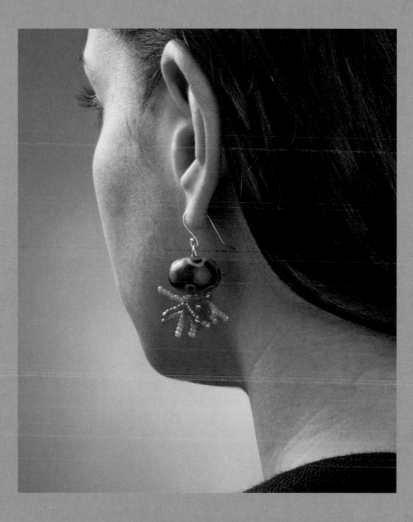

4 Make a branch extending from the bottom of the large bead by stringing 8 red beads, skipping over the last bead, and going back through 6 beads. Gently pull the thread taut. Make a twig on the branch by stringing 8 red beads, skipping over the last bead, and going back through 6 beads. Gently pull the thread taut.

5 Make another twig by stringing 6 red beads, skipping over the last bead, and going back through 5 beads. Gently pull the thread taut. Draw the thread back through the beads that make up the base of the branch and through the large bead. Loop the thread over the ring and draw it back through the large bead. Repeat with orange beads to make another branch (Figure C).

C

6 Repeat step 5, alternating between red and orange beads, to make several branches. When the last branch is complete, tie the thread in a secure knot and reinforce with a dot of superglue. Wait for the superglue to dry, then cut the thread close to the knot.

7 Repeat steps 1–6 to make the second earring.

8 To finish, attach ear wires to the metal rings.

Octopus Earrings

These playful earrings can be made with one, two, three, or even four colors of beads. Use as many color combinations as you dare!

Materials

Beading thread

Two 2 x 2½-inch pieces of Lycra

Seed beads, size 11, green, blue, red, orange, pink

Pair of small hoop earrings

Tools

Beading needle, size 11 or 12

Scissors

Directions

1 Thread the needle with a comfortable length of thread, double it, and tie both ends together.

2 Tightly roll a piece of Lycra into a 2-inch cylinder and sew the seam (Figure A). Roll the cylinder into a spiral shape and sew the seam (Figure B).

3 Insert the needle into the spiral so it comes out on the top of the spiral, near the middle. String 8–10 beads, alternating between green and blue, until you reach the bottom of the spiral, near the middle. Insert the needle and push through so that it comes out at the top, beside the first column of beads (Figure C).

(continued on page 52)

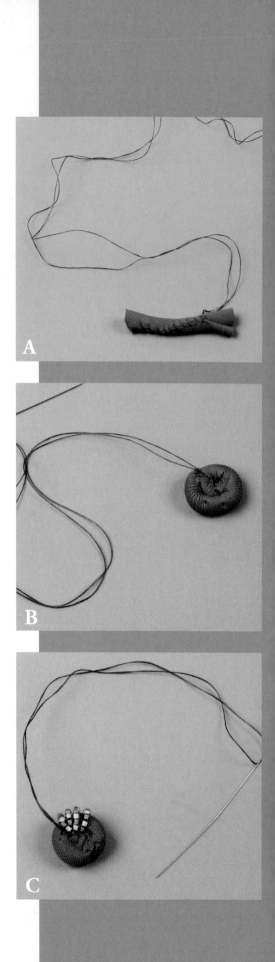

A

B

C

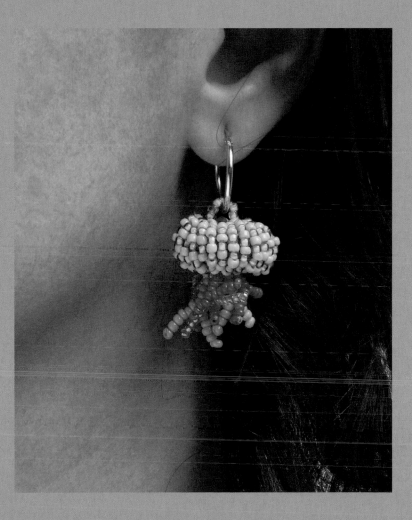

4 Repeat step 3 until the entire spiral is wrapped in beads, then insert the needle and push through so that it comes out at the top of the spiral, near the middle. String 8 green beads, then insert the needle into the spiral to form a loop (Figure D). Make a second loop beside the first.

5 Make a branch extending from the bottom of the beaded spiral by inserting the needle so that it comes out at the bottom of the beaded spiral, near the middle. String 12 red beads, skip over the last bead, and go back through 6 beads. Gently pull the thread taut.

6 Make a twig on the branch by stringing 6 red beads, skipping over the last bead, and going back through 5 beads. Gently pull the thread taut. Draw the thread back through the beads that make up the base of the branch and into the beaded spiral. Repeat with orange beads to make another branch (Figure E).

7 Repeat steps 5–6, alternating between red, orange, and pink beads, to make several branches. When the last branch is complete, draw the thread into the beaded spiral, tie in a secure knot, and cut close to the knot.

8 Repeat steps 1–7 to make the second earring.

9 To finish, attach a small hoop earring through the double loop on the top of each earring.

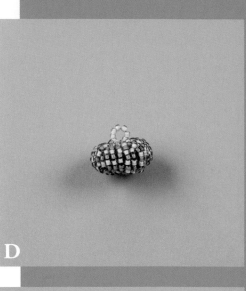

D

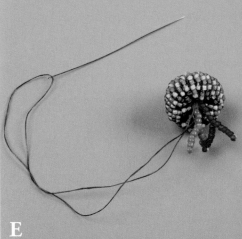

E

Porcupine Ball Earrings

These earrings are an easy way to accessorize! No two earrings have to be the same color, so create them to mix and match.

Materials

Beading thread

Two 2½-inch squares of Lycra

Seed beads, size 6, green and blue

Seed beads, size 11, green and blue

Pair of ear wires

Tools

Beading needle, size 11 or 12

Scissors

Directions

1 Thread the needle with a comfortable length of thread, double it, and tie both ends together.

2 Fold a piece of Lycra in half into a rectangle, then in half to make a small square. Fold all four corners into the middle of the square to make a smaller square, and sew the corners together (Figure A). Continue to fold and sew opposite corners into the middle, stretching and shaping the Lycra as you go (Figure B), until you have a small ball (Figure C).

(continued on page 56)

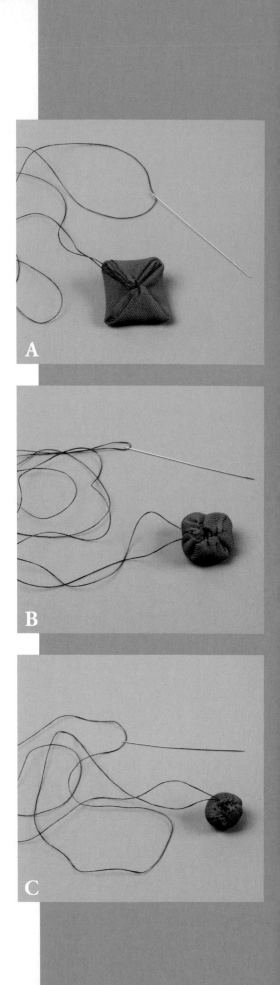

3 Insert the needle through the ball and string a large green bead followed by a small blue bead. Loop the thread around the blue bead, draw it back through the green bead, and insert into the ball. Push the needle out close to the newly attached beads and pull gently to secure the beads against the ball (Figure D).

4 Repeat step 3 until the whole ball is covered with beads. Push the needle out at any point on the ball and string 1 large green bead, then 15 small blue beads. Make a loop with 6 of the blue beads, draw the needle back through 9 blue beads and the green bead, and insert it into the ball.

5 Push the needle out, gently pull the thread to secure the beads, and tie a secure knot close to the ball. Cut the thread close to the knot (Figure E).

6 Repeat steps 1–5, using the reverse combi–nation of blue and green beads, to make the second earring.

7 To finish, attach ear wires through the loop on each earring.

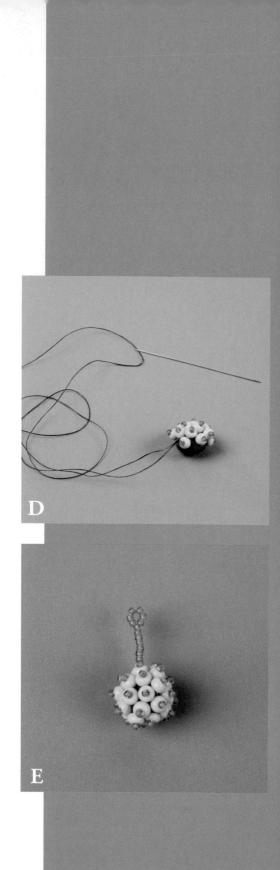

D

E

Icicle Earrings

Warm your ears on a cold winter's day with these dazzling dangly earrings. Make them as long as you like and add an abundance of icicles for a wonderful wintry look.

Materials

Beading thread

Two 2 x 2½-inch pieces of Lycra

Seed beads, size 11, variety of wintry colors (white, pearl, gray, silver, transparent)

Seed beads, size 8, various shades of blue and green

Pair of small hoop earrings

Tools

Beading needle, size 11 or 12

Scissors

Directions

1 Thread the needle with a comfortable length of thread, double it, and tie both ends together.

2 Tightly roll a piece of Lycra into a 2-inch cylinder and sew the seam (Figure A). Roll the cylinder into a spiral shape and sew the seam (Figure B).

3 Insert the needle into the spiral so it comes out on the top of the spiral, near the middle. String 8–10 small white beads until you reach the bottom of the spiral, near the middle. Insert the needle and push through so that it comes out at the top, beside the first column of beads (Figure C).

(continued on page 60)

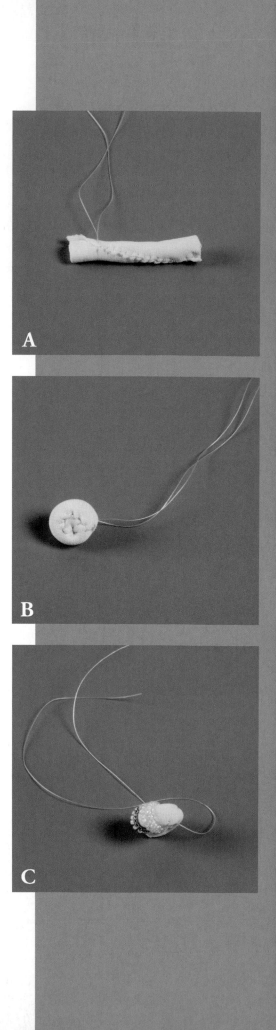

A

B

C

4 Repeat step 3 until the entire spiral is wrapped in beads; feel free to integrate a column of gray or silver beads every now and then, if you like. Insert the needle and push through so that it comes out at the bottom of the beaded spiral, near the middle. String 20 small wintry beads, 1 large color bead, and 1 small wintry bead. Skip over the last bead, and go back through 9 beads. Gently pull the thread taut. Make a twig on the branch by stringing 12 small wintry beads, 1 large color bead, and 1 wintry bead. Skip over the last bead, and go back through 9 beads. Gently pull the thread taut.

5 Make another twig by stringing 10 small wintry beads, 1 large color bead, and 1 wintry bead. Skip over the last bead, and go back through 6 beads. Gently pull the thread taut. Make another twig by stringing 6 small wintry beads, 1 large color bead, and 1 wintry bead. Skip over the last bead, and go back through all of the beads that make up the base of the branch and into the beaded spiral.

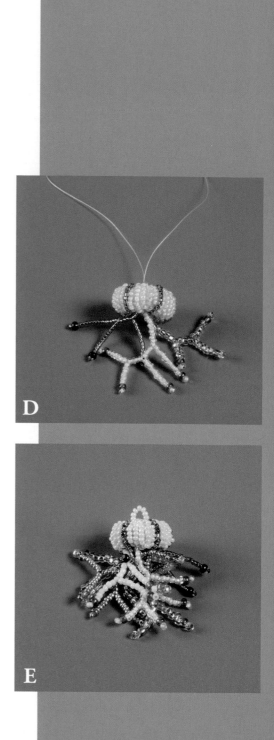

D

E

6 Repeat steps 4–5 to make several branches so that the earring is lush with icicles (Figure D). When the last branch is complete, draw the thread into the beaded spiral and push through so that it comes out at the top of the spiral, near the middle. String 8 white beads, then insert the needle into the spiral to form a loop. Push the thread through the spiral, tie in a secure knot, and cut close to the knot (Figure E).

7 Repeat steps 1–6 to make the second earring.

8 To finish, attach a small hoop earring through the double loop on the top of each earring.

Bracelets

*Thick or thin,
bangle-style or clasped,
colorful beaded bracelets
liven up every wrist.
Measure the bracelet
against your wrist as you
work to make sure it's
just the right size.*

Tinsel Bracelet

No celebration is complete without tinsel, and this tinsel bracelet is its own celebration of color!

Materials

Sixty-five 1-inch head pins

Glass beads, variety of shapes and colors

Roll of sturdy rubber thread

Seed beads, size 6, variety of colors

Superglue

Tools

Round-nose pliers

Wire cutters

Scissors

A

Directions

1 To make a piece of tinsel, string 2–4 glass beads on a head pin. Use round-nose pliers to bend the sharp end of the head pin into a closed double loop and use wire cutters to cut off any remaining wire. Combine a variety of shapes and colors on each pin, so that each piece of tinsel is a little different (Figure A). Repeat to make 65 pieces of tinsel.

(continued on page 66)

2 Cut an 18-inch piece of rubber thread from the roll and fold in half. String a piece of tinsel onto the double thread through the loop you made in the head pin.

3 String a seed bead then two more pieces of tinsel, another seed bead, and two more pieces of tinsel (Figure B). Take care that the pieces of tinsel don't slide off the thread as you work.

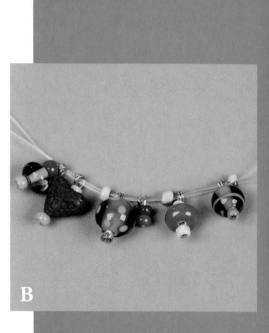

B

4 Continue alternating between seed beads and tinsel, measuring against your wrist as you go, until the bracelet is the right length.

5 To finish, draw together both ends of the rubber thread, tie them in a tight double knot, and reinforce with a dot of superglue. Wait for the superglue to dry, then cut the thread close to the knot.

Beaded Bangle

Jazz up any outfit with this bold bangle-style bracelet. Make it with wild colors or subtle colors—or why not one of each?

Materials
Beading thread

8 x 9-inch piece of Lycra

Seed beads, size 6, variety of colors

Seed beads, size 11, variety of colors

Tools
Beading needle, size 11 or 12

Straight pins

Scissors

Directions

1 Thread the needle with a comfortable length of thread, double it, and tie both ends together.

2 Tightly roll the Lycra into a 9-inch cylinder with a diameter of about ½ inch and sew the seam. Use straight pins to hold the fabric in place if necessary (Figure A). Sew the ends of the cylinder together to make a large ring (Figure B). Make sure the ring fits easily onto your wrist, remembering that the size of the hole in the middle of the ring will be reduced after you add the beads.

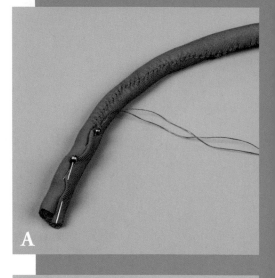

A

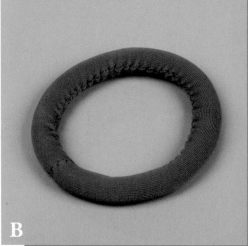

B

(continued on page 70)

3 Insert the needle through the fabric and string a large bead followed by a small bead of a different color. Loop the thread around the small bead, draw it back through the large bead, and insert into the fabric.

4 Push the needle out close to the newly attached beads and pull gently to secure the beads against the fabric (Figure C).

5 Repeat step 4 until the bracelet is covered with beads.

6 To finish, tie a small knot in the thread and cut the thread close to the fabric.

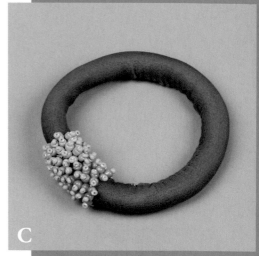

Note: *If you are working with a particularly remarkable fabric, just cover part of the bracelet with beads and leave some of it undecorated.*

Balls of Beads Bracelet

Adjust the size of the balls in this bracelet according to your style—smaller balls make a more elegant bracelet while larger balls give the bracelet a funkier look.

Materials

Beading thread

Thirteen 2½-inch squares of Lycra

Seed beads, size 6, variety of colors

Seed beads, size 11, variety of colors

Tools

Beading needle, size 11 or 12

Scissors

Directions

1 Thread the needle with a comfortable length of thread, double it, and tie both ends together.

2 Fold a piece of Lycra in half into a rectangle, then in half to make a small square. Fold all four corners into the middle of the square to make a smaller square, and sew the corners together (Figure A). Continue to fold and sew opposite corners into the middle, stretching and shaping the Lycra as you go (Figure B), until you have a ball with a diameter of about ½ inch (Figure C). Repeat to make 13 balls, or as many as you'll need to make your bracelet.

(continued on page 74)

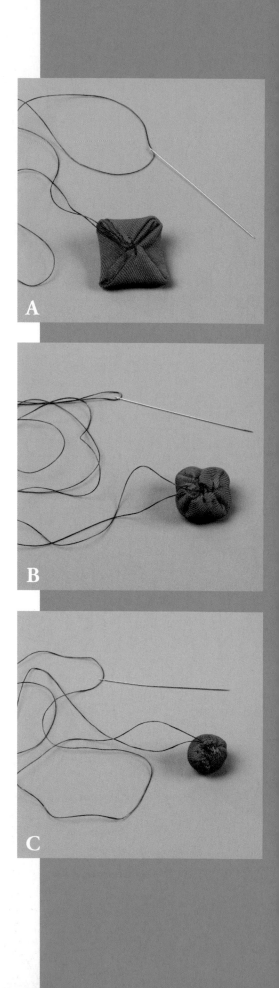

3 Insert the needle through a ball and string a large blue bead followed by a small yellow bead. Loop the thread around the yellow bead, draw it back through the blue bead, and insert into the ball. Push the needle out close to the newly attached beads and pull gently to secure the beads against the ball (Figure D).

4 Repeat step 3 until the whole ball is covered with beads, then tie a secure knot close to the ball and cut the thread.

5 Repeat steps 3–4, using different color combinations, to cover all 13 balls in beads.

6 Thread the needle with a 28-inch piece of thread, double it, and tie both ends together.

7 Insert the needle through a beaded ball and push it out on the opposite side. String 5 small beads, then string another beaded ball (Figure E).

8 Continue alternating between beaded balls and small beads, measuring against your wrist as you go, until the bracelet is the right length.

9 To finish, draw the thread out of the last ball, string 5 small beads, then insert into the first ball. Sew a small stitch to secure, tie a knot close to the ball, and cut the thread.

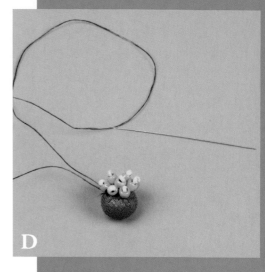

D

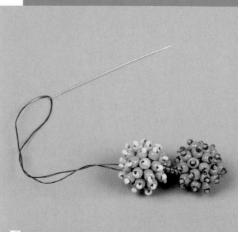

E

Note: *The number of balls you need for this bracelet depends upon the size of the balls and the size of your wrist. Measure the balls against your wrist at the beginning, so that you don't find yourself with too few balls as you near the end. If you have any extra balls, attach a pin back to make a matching brooch or add ear wires to make a pair of earrings.*

Winter Wonderland Bracelet

Celebrate the world's whitest season by using an assortment of wintry colors in this project. Adding matte, translucent, opaque, and glossy beads increases the bracelet's brilliance and beauty.

Materials

300 1-inch head pins

Seed beads, sizes 6, 8, and 11, variety of wintry colors (white, pearl, gray, silver)

Seed beads, sizes 6 and 8, variety of colors (blue, green, turquoise)

Roll of sturdy rubber thread

Superglue

Tools

Round-nose pliers

Wire cutters

Directions

1 Make a piece of snowy tinsel by stringing 7–8 wintry beads, in various sizes, on a head pin. Use round-nose pliers to bend the sharp end of the head pin into a closed loop and use wire cutters to cut off any remaining wire. Repeat to make 100 pieces of tinsel.

2 Make a piece of color tinsel by stringing 1 color bead then 4–7 wintry beads on a head pin. Use various sizes of beads and vary the number of beads you put on each head pin. Use round-nose pliers to bend the sharp end of the head pin into a closed loop and use wire cutters to cut off any remaining wire (Figure A). Repeat to make 200 pieces.

A

(continued on page 78)

3 Cut two 24-inch pieces of rubber thread. Your bracelet will actually be much shorter than this, but working with long pieces of thread makes it easier to keep the tinsel on the thread as you work.

4 Start stringing tinsel onto one piece of rubber thread in the following pattern: Thread one piece of snowy tinsel then two pieces of color tinsel. Repeat this order, taking care to place different lengths of tinsel beside each other (Figure B). Watch that the pieces of tinsel don't slide off the thread as you work.

5 Repeat step 4 until each piece of thread contains 150 pieces of tinsel (Figure C).

6 Twist together the two pieces of thread (Figure D). Work carefully to make sure that none of the tinsel slides off the ends.

7 To finish, tie all four ends of rubber thread together in a secure double knot and reinforce with a drop of superglue. Wait for the superglue to dry, then cut the thread close to the knot.

Note: *For a single-strand bracelet, make 50 pieces of wintry tinsel and 100 pieces of color tinsel and string them onto a single piece of rubber thread.*

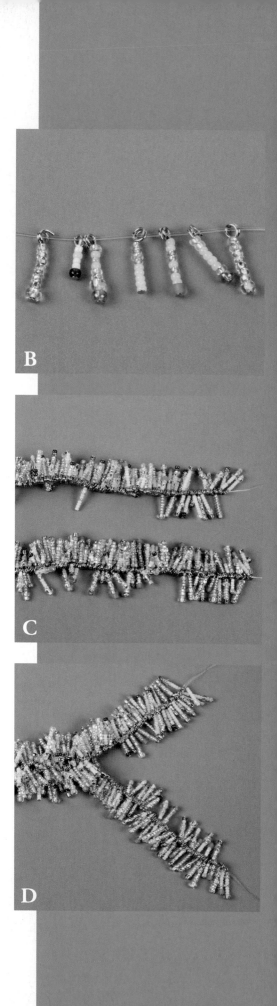

B

C

D

Brooches and Pendants

Pinned to a lapel, scarf, or hat, or set off on a colorful ribbon, these designs are relatively simple and remarkably versatile.

Heart Pillow Brooch

This heartwarming brooch will bring a smile to anyone who makes it, wears it, or simply sees it! Choose the colors according to your heart's desire!

Materials

Beading thread

Pin back

Heart-shaped appliqué

Seed beads, size 6, orange, pink

Seed beads, size 11, pink, orange

Tools

Scissors

Beading needle, size 11 or 12

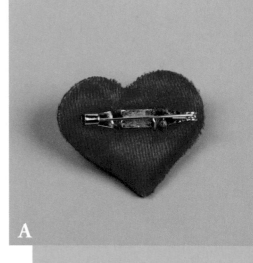

A

Directions

1 Thread the needle with a comfortable length of thread, double it, and tie both ends together.

2 Sew the pin back to the back of the appliqué (Figure A).

(continued on page 84)

3 Insert the needle into the appliqué and string a large orange bead followed by a small pink bead. Loop the thread around the pink bead, draw it back through the orange bead, and insert into the appliqué. Push the needle out close to the newly attached beads and pull gently to secure the beads against the appliqué (Figure B).

4 Repeat step 3 until both sides of the appliqué are covered in beads, switching colors when you are halfway done so that you use large pink beads with small orange ones. To finish, tie the thread in a knot close to the pillow and cut close to the knot.

B

Note: *If you can't find an appliqué you like, or if you prefer to make the base for this brooch by hand, that's fine too. Just draw a heart (or whatever shape you like) on a 2½-inch square of paper and cut it out. Trace the shape onto two 2½-inch squares of fabric and cut them out. Sew together the edges of the fabric, leaving one end open to stuff. Fill with just enough stuffing to make a small pillow and sew closed.*

Ellipse Coral Brooch

This design is inspired by the underwater world of coral, anemones, and sea snails. Bright and versatile, it can liven up a warm winter hat or light autumn scarf.

Materials

Beading thread

2 x 2¾-inch piece of Lycra

Pin back

Seed beads, size 6, green, orange, red, pink

Tools

Beading needle, size 11 or 12

Scissors

Directions

1 Thread the needle with a comfortable length of thread, double it, and tie both ends together.

2 Tightly roll the Lycra into a 2¾-inch cylinder with a diameter of about ¼ inch and sew the seam (Figure A). Sew the ends of the cylinder together to make a ring shape (Figure B).

3 Press together the top and bottom of the ring to make an ellipse shape and sew together, closing up the space in the middle (Figure C).

(continued on page 88)

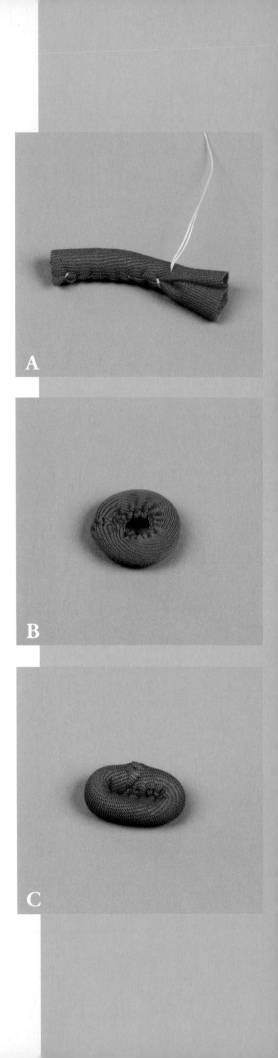

A

B

C

4 Sew the pin back to the back of the ellipse (Figure D).

5 Insert the needle so that it comes out at the front in the center of the ellipse. String 12–15 green beads, or as many as you need to reach the center on the other side of the ellipse. Insert the needle at the back of the ellipse and push through so that it comes out at the front, beside the first column of beads (Figure E).

6 Repeat step 5 until the entire ellipse is wrapped in beads.

7 Insert the needle into the ellipse so that it comes out on the rim. Make a branch of beads by stringing 10 orange beads, skipping over the last bead, and going back through 6 beads. Gently pull the thread taut. Make a twig by stringing 6 orange beads, skipping over the last bead, and going back through 10 beads, 5 of which are part of the twig, and 5 which were the base beads. Insert the needle into the ellipse and push out close to the branch. Repeat with red and pink beads to make more branches (Figure F).

8 Repeat step 7 until the ellipse is surrounded by branches of beads. To finish, tie a secure knot and cut the thread close to the knot.

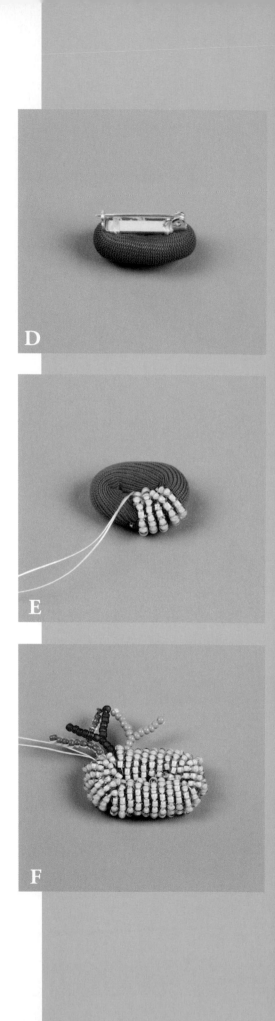

D

E

F

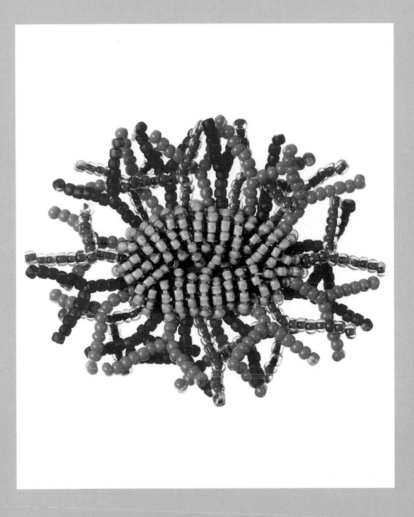

Open Heart Brooch

This brooch will open anyone's heart to beading. Perfect for Valentine's Day, Mother's Day, or any other day of the year.

Materials

Beading thread

Two 5-inch pieces of thin, flexible wire

Two 3 x 4-inch pieces of Lycra

Pin back

Seed beads, size 6, pink and red

Seed beads, size 11, green

Tools

Beading needle, size 11 or 12

Straight pins

Scissors

Wire cutters

Directions

1 Thread the needle with a comfortable length of thread, double it, and tie both ends together.

2 Place one piece of wire along the 4-inch edge of a piece of Lycra and tightly roll the Lycra into a cylinder. Sew together the seam using straight pins to hold the fabric in place if necessary (Figure A). Use wire cutters to trim the ends of the wires so that they are flush with the Lycra and bend the cylinder to form half of a heart (Figure B).

3 Repeat step 2 with the other piece of wire and Lycra and sew the ends of both cylinders together to form a heart shape (Figure C).

(continued on page 92)

A

B

C

4 Sew the pin back to the heart. Insert the needle through the fabric and string a pink bead followed by a green bead. Loop the thread around the green bead, draw it back through the pink bead, and insert into the fabric.

5 Push the needle out close to the newly attached beads and pull gently to secure the beads against the fabric.

6 Repeat step 5 on both the front and the back of the brooch (Figures D1 and D2). Switch from pink beads to red beads when you are about halfway done. To finish, tie the thread in a secure knot close to the fabric and cut close to the knot.

Note: *Shape the pieces of wire into any form you like to create animals, symbols, letters, or abstract designs.*

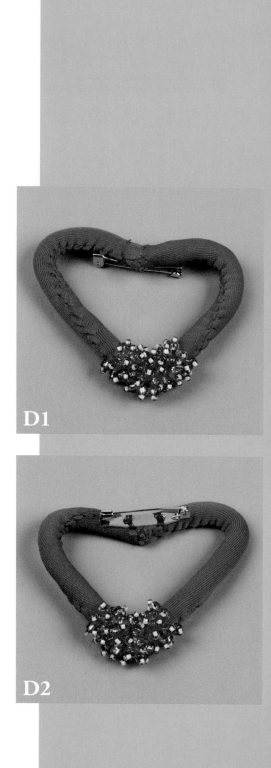

D1

D2

Sunburst Pendant

This colorful sunburst can be worn as a pendant or a brooch. Use any colors under the sun that inspire you.

Materials

Beading thread

2¾ x 4-inch piece of Lycra

Pin back

Seed beads, size 6, green

Seed beads, size 11, various shades of blue and green

31-inch ribbon

Tools

Beading needle, size 11 or 12

Scissors

Directions

1 Thread the needle with a comfortable length of thread, double it, and tie both ends together.

2 Tightly roll the Lycra into a 2¾-inch cylinder with a diameter of about ⅓ inch and sew the seam (Figure A). Sew the ends of the cylinder together to make a ring shape (Figure B). Sew the pin back to the back of the ring (Figure C).

(continued on page 96)

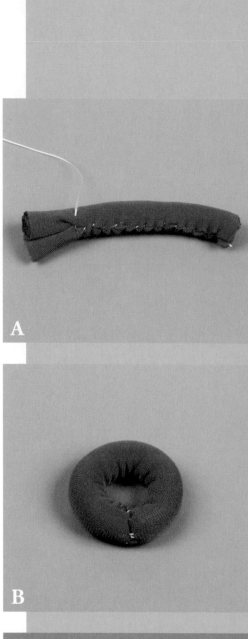

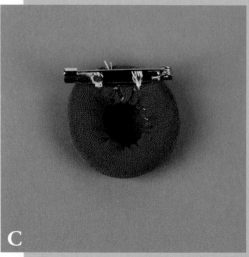

3 Insert the needle through the ring and string a large green bead followed by a small blue bead. Loop the thread around the blue bead, draw it back through the green bead and insert into the ring. Push the needle out close to the newly attached beads and pull gently to secure the beads against the ring (Figure D).

4 Repeat step 3 until the whole ring is covered with beads.

5 Insert the needle into the ring so it comes out on the rim. Make a branch of beads by stringing 8 small blue beads, skipping over the last bead, and going back through 6 beads. Gently pull the thread taut. Make a twig on the branch by stringing 8 more blue beads, skipping over the last bead, and going back through 6 beads. Gently pull the thread taut.

6 Make another twig by stringing 6 more blue beads, skipping over the last bead, and going back through 5 beads. Draw the thread back through the beads that make up the base of the branch and into the ring. Push the needle out close to the branch and pull gently to secure the branch. Repeat to make several branches using various shades of blue and green beads (Figure E).

7 Repeat steps 5–6 until the ring is surrounded by branches of beads, then tie a secure knot and cut the thread close to the knot.

8 To finish, sew together the ends of the ribbon and pin the sunburst to the middle.

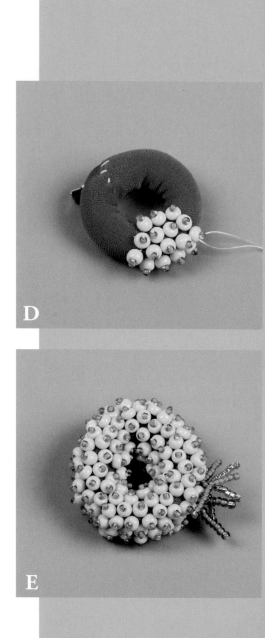

D

E

Snowflake Brooch

Natural snowflakes are fleetingly beautiful; this delicate brooch retains its charm throughout the season, and all year long.

Materials

Beading thread

2 x 2½-inch piece of Lycra

Pin back

Seed beads, size 11, variety of wintry colors (pearl, gray, silver, transparent)

Seed beads, size 6, variety of colors (orange, peach, pink)

Tools

Beading needle, size 11 or 12

Scissors

Directions

1 Thread the needle with a comfortable length of thread, double it, and tie both ends together.

2 Tightly roll the Lycra into a 2-inch cylinder and sew the seam (Figure A). Sew the ends of the cylinder together to make a ring shape (Figure B). Sew the pin back to the back of the ring (Figure C).

(continued on page 100)

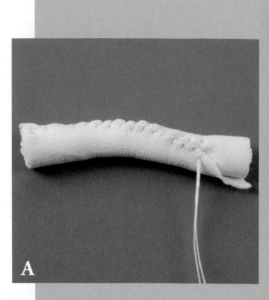

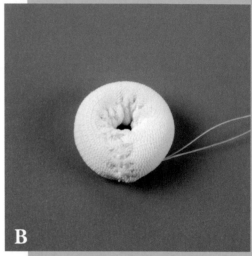

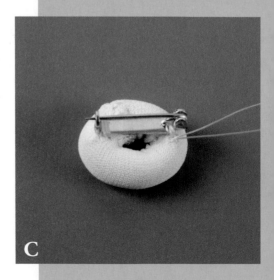

3 Insert the needle so that it comes out at the bottom of the ring. String 25–30 small pearl beads and bring the needle up through the middle of the ring, wrapping the ring in beads. Continue stringing beads and wrapping them around the ring, inserting the needle into the Lycra every now and then to secure the beads in place (Figure D).

4 Continue wrapping the ring until it is totally covered in beads.

5 Insert the needle into the ring so it comes out near the rim and begin making branches to surround the ring. One type of branch is shorter, and made with only small beads. To make these branches, string 8 pearl beads, skip over the last bead, and go back through 7 beads. Gently pull the thread taut. Make a twig on the branch by stringing 7 pearl beads, skipping over the last bead, and going back through all the beads that make up the base of the branch and into the ring. The other type of branch is longer, and includes a large color bead near the tip. To make these branches, string 13 small gray beads, 1 large color bead, and 1 small gray bead. Skip over the last bead and go back through 7 beads. Gently pull the thread taut. Make a twig on the branch by stringing 6 small gray beads, 1 large color bead, and 1 small gray bead. Skip over the last bead and go back through all the beads that make up the base of the branch and into the ring.

6 Repeat step 5, alternating between small pearl branches and larger gray or silver branches with orange, peach, or pink tips (Figure E). Having many branches is what gives this design its lush, plentiful look, so try clustering the branches richly around the ring. Tie a secure knot and cut the thread close to the knot.

D

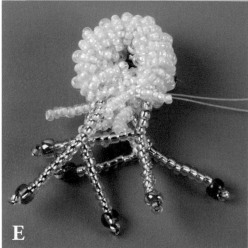

E

Advanced Projects

Once you've mastered the basic techniques, give these projects a whirl. More time-intensive than the rest, but the results are simply dazzling.

Radiant Ring Bracelet

With bright vibrant colors and a triple layer of beads,
this bracelet adds radiance to any outfit.

Materials

Beading thread

Fifteen $2\frac{3}{4}$ x $3\frac{1}{2}$-inch pieces of Lycra

Seed beads, size 6, variety of colors

Seed beads, size 8, variety of colors

Seed beads, size 11, variety of colors

Roll of sturdy rubber thread

Superglue

Tools

Beading needle, size 11 or 12

Scissors

Directions

1 Thread the needle with a comfortable length of thread, double it, and tie both ends together.

2 Tightly roll a piece of Lycra into a $2\frac{3}{4}$-inch cylinder and sew together the seam. Sew the ends of the cylinder together to make a ring shape. Repeat to make 15 rings, or as many as you'll need to make your bracelet.

3 Insert the needle into one of the rings and string a large bead of one color, a medium bead of another color, then a small bead of a third color. Loop the thread around the small bead, draw it back through the medium and large beads, and insert it into the ring.

(continued on page 106)

4 Push the needle out close to the newly attached beads and pull gently to secure the beads against the ring.

5 Repeat steps 3–4 until the exterior of the ring is covered with beads. Tie a secure knot close to the ring and cut the thread.

6 Repeat steps 3–5 to cover all 15 rings in beads.

7 Unwind about 9 inches of rubber thread from the roll, but don't cut the thread. String the beaded rings onto the thread, measuring against your wrist as you go, until the bracelet is the right length.

8 To finish, draw together both ends of the rubber thread, tie them in a tight double knot, and reinforce with a dot of superglue. Wait for the superglue to dry, then cut close to the knot.

Gumdrop Necklace

This necklace is simply delectable. Use different colors of gumdrops to sweeten up your jewelry collection!

Materials

Beading thread

Thirty 1½-inch squares of Lycra

Seed beads, size 6, variety of colors

Seed beads, size 11, variety of colors

2½-inch square of Lycra

Tools

Beading needle, size 11 or 12

Scissors

Directions

1 Thread the needle with a comfortable length of thread, double it, and tie both ends together.

2 Fold a piece of Lycra in half along the diagonal to make a triangle. Fold each triangle in half, and again in half, to make a smaller triangle. Roll one of the corners in to make a small gumdrop shape and sew together the seam. Repeat to make 30 gumdrops.

3 Insert the needle through a gumdrop and string a large bead followed by a small bead of a different color. Loop the thread around the small bead, and draw it back through the larger bead and into the fabric. Push the needle out close to the newly attached beads and pull gently to secure the beads against the fabric. Repeat until the whole gumdrop is covered with beads.

(continued on page 110)

4 Repeat step 3 to cover all 30 gumdrops in beads.

5 Thread the needle with a comfortable length of thread, double it, and tie both ends together. String the gumdrops until you have the right length for your necklace. Tie a double knot and cut the thread close to the knot.

6 To make the clasp, fold the 2½-inch square of Lycra into a rectangle, then in half to make a small square. Fold all four corners into the middle of the square to make a smaller square, and sew the corners together. Continue to fold and sew opposite corners into the middle, stretching and shaping the Lycra as you go, until you have a small ball. Cover the ball with beads using the technique described in step 3.

7 To attach the clasp, thread the needle and insert it through the first gumdrop. String 10 small beads, then draw the thread through the beaded ball. String 10 more beads, then insert the needle into the same gumdrop and push through to the other side. Tie the thread in a secure knot and cut close to the gumdrop.

8 To make the loop, thread the needle and insert it into the last gumdrop. String 30 beads, or as many as necessary for making a loop into which the clasp will fit comfortably and securely. Insert the needle into the same gumdrop and push through to the other side. Tie the thread in a secure knot and cut close to the gumdrop.

Medallion Necklace

Make multiple statements with multiple medallions! Each different shape adds a new dimension to your look.

Materials

Beading thread

Twenty-two 2-inch squares of Lycra

Stuffing

Colored ribbon

Seed beads, size 6, variety of colors

Seed beads, size 11, variety of colors

Small buttons

1 round shoelace or thin rope

Tools

Beading needle, size 11 or 12

Scissors

Directions

1 Thread the needle with a comfortable length of thread, double it, and tie both ends together.

2 Make several small pillows in various shapes in the following manner: Trace a shape onto two pieces of Lycra and cut out. Sew together the edges of the fabric, leaving one end open to fill. Fill with just enough stuffing to make a small pillow and sew closed.

3 Sew a loop of colored ribbon onto each medallion. This loop will be used to string the medallions onto the necklace, so make sure it fits nicely over the shoelace.

(continued on page 114)

4 Insert the needle into a medallion and string a large bead followed by a small bead of a different color. Loop the thread around the smaller bead, and draw it back through the larger bead and into the fabric. Push the needle out close to the newly attached beads and pull gently to secure the beads against the medallion.

5 Repeat step 4 until the medallion is covered in beads. Use your imagination to add buttons, pieces of ribbon, and diverse types of beads using various techniques.

6 Repeat steps 4–5 until all of the medallions are covered in beads.

7 String the medallions onto the shoelace and secure into place with a single stitch.

8 To make the clasp, sew a small piece of cloth onto either end of the necklace. Sew a button onto the cloth at one end of the necklace and cut a buttonhole into the cloth at the other end of the necklace.

> **Note:** *Instead of making your own medallions in step 2, you can also use store-bought appliqués, available at many craft stores and hobby shops.*

Razzle Dazzle Ring Necklace

While making this necklace takes quite a bit of time, the final product is no less than magnificent. This is a perfect project for any long holiday.

Materials

Beading thread

Forty-one 2-inch squares of Lycra

Seed beads, size 11, variety of colors

1 long round shoelace or thin rope

Tools

Beading needle, size 11 or 12

Scissors

Directions

1 Thread the needle with a comfortable length of thread, double it, and tie both ends together.

2 Roll one of the pieces of Lycra into a cylinder and sew the seam. Sew the ends of the cylinder together to make a ring shape and sew the seam. Repeat to make 41 ring shapes.

3 Insert the needle through a ring so it comes out at the top of the ring. String 6–10 beads, or as many as you need to wrap the ring. Insert the needle at the bottom, so that you have a column of beads that runs the length of the ring. Push the needle through so that it comes out at the top of the ring, beside the first column of beads. Repeat until the whole ring is wrapped in beads.

4 Repeat step 3, using various combinations of colors, until all 41 rings are covered in beads.

(continued on page 118)

5 String 40 beaded rings onto the shoelace, reserving one of the rings for the clasp. Leave about 7½ inches at one end and 4½ inches on the other end to make the loop and the clasp.

6 To make the loop, bend the 7½-inch end of the shoelace to form a 2-inch loop and sew the loop into place. To wrap the shoelace with beads, thread the needle and insert into the shoelace just after the last beaded ring. String small beads onto the thread and wrap tightly around the shoelace, wrapping the area of the loop as well. Anchor the string of beads into place every now and then by inserting the needle into the shoelace. When this side is wrapped, insert the needle into the shoelace, tie a secure knot, and cut close to the knot.

7 To make the clasp, sew the remaining beaded ring at the other end of the shoelace. Wrap this side of the shoelace in small beads using the technique described in step 6.

8 To make the fringes that stick out of the clasp, insert the thread into the end of the shoelace and push out in the center of the clasp. String 5 beads onto the thread, skip over the last bead, and go back through 4 beads. Anchor the thread in the shoelace and repeat to make several fringes.

Rainbow of Rings Necklace

Get ready for a rainbow of compliments! The addition of beaded ropes between each ring in this necklace adds a dramatic, somewhat exotic effect.

Materials

Beading thread

Fourteen 2³/₄ x 3¹/₂-inch pieces of Lycra

Seed beads, size 6, variety of colors

Seed beads, size 11, variety of colors

Tools

Beading needle, size 11 or 12

Scissors

Directions

1 Thread the needle with a comfortable length of thread, double it, and tie both ends together.

2 Tightly roll a piece of Lycra into a 2³/₄-inch cylinder and sew the seam. Sew the ends of the cylinder together to make a large ring. Repeat to make 14 rings.

3 Insert the needle into one of the rings and string a large bead followed by a small bead of a different color. Loop the thread around the small bead, draw it back through the large bead, and insert it into the ring.

(continued on page 122)

4 Push the needle out close to the newly attached beads and pull gently to secure the beads against the ring.

5 Repeat steps 3–4 until the exterior of the ring is covered with beads. Tie a secure knot close to the ring and cut the thread.

6 Repeat steps 3–5, using different color combinations, to cover all the rings in beads.

7 Cut 9 pieces of thread so that they are each about 40 inches long. Tie them together at one end with a secure double knot.

8 String each thread separately with 35 large beads, then string one beaded ring onto all the threads together.

9 Repeat step 8 until the necklace is the right length. To finish, tie the ends of the necklace together.

Index

Metric Equivalents					
inches	cm	inches	cm	inches	cm
1	2.54	11	27.94	21	53.34
2	5.08	12	30.48	22	55.88
3	7.62	13	33.02	23	58.42
4	10.16	14	35.56	24	60.96
5	12.7	15	38.1	30	76.2
6	15.24	16	40.64	36	91.44
7	17.78	17	43.18	42	106.68
8	20.32	18	45.72	48	121.92
9	22.86	19	48.26	54	137.16
10	25.4	20	50.8	60	152.4